Praise for *Mut*

A deeply perceptive poet with a ....
world, Geraldine Mitchell's poems both offer a timely
warning that the planet is mortal, and offer a reassuring
reminder of life's cyclical nature. These poems are a
stunning sketch of a world that is a place of great beauty
and great challenge. Mitchell reflects on a life marked out
in distances – between cities; the sky to the sea; the spaces
between the paw prints of a wolf; masterfully excavating
extraordinary glimpses of the ordinary. These poems
listen, watch, and unearth a voice for the voiceless – from
Mayo and far beyond – Mitchell explores humans at their
most vulnerable. And when our *systems fail*, the
counterpressures of love and humanity are all we have. An
assured and powerful collection, *Mute/Unmute* is
contemporary poetry at its finest.

– Elaine Feeney

There's a lot of darkness here, but that darkness never feels
depressing. There's too much light in the language, too
much craft and passion in the making. Mitchell has
dreamed up a black tulip of a book that can surprise us
with brightness as it pours out the dark.

– Theodore Deppe

As political as it is personal and as global as it is local, this
intensely moving collection pays homage to people and
place with sensuous detail and profound empathy.

– Jane Clarke

MUTE/UNMUTE

Geraldine Mitchell

MUTE/UNMUTE

ARLEN
HOUSE

Mute/Unmute

is published in 2020 by
ARLEN HOUSE
42 Grange Abbey Road
Baldoyle, Dublin 13, Ireland
Phone: 00 353 86 8360236
arlenhouse@gmail.com
arlenhouse.blogspot.com

978–1–85132–246–6, *paperback*

Distributed internationally by
SYRACUSE UNIVERSITY PRESS
621 Skytop Road, Suite 110
Syracuse, NY 13244–5290
Phone: 315–443–5534
Fax: 315–443–5545
supress@syr.edu
syracuseuniversitypress.syr.edu

Typesetting by Arlen House

cover image:
'Garden of Gethsemane'
by Mags Duffy
is reproduced courtesy of the artist

CONTENTS

for Macha

MUTE/UNMUTE

Pour Out the Dark

I

TEST

Tell me what you know about the Dandelion.

Tell me what you know about the Bee.

Tell me what you know about the Sun, Moon and Stars
        and the Sea's tassled Blanket, the Fish that
        swim through it, its Weave.

Tell me what you know about the Open Coast,
        the swallowing Brine brimming
        its rocky Shore, the Birds' rich textured
        Concert, all Feather and Beak and itching
        Parasites.

Tell me what you know about the Circulation of the
        Blood, how as you lie on the grassy Crust
        of a windy Cliff, you trust your Heart
        will thump you into another Day.

Tell me what you know.

ISLAND LIFE

I don't like too much social life anyway. It is gossip
and bad white wine.

– Edna O'Brien

1

All summer they sit, like cakes
in a cake shop window, dusted
with promise, treats for a cloudless
day, fair-weather destinations,
notional ports in a storm.

2

She backs her life
close to the edge
along a road
that ends in a tidal
cul de sac stitched up
by gannets and terns.

3

No man is an island but
she is no man so perhaps
she'll become one, an island
compact and self-contained,
three waterfalls, an orchard,
a herd of feral goats, sixteen
types of wild orchid to lure
hatted experts in summer
                    then wait
for the season to change, for
the island to empty, the stillness
of salt-splashed winter months.

4

You live in a beautiful part of the world,
so remote.
I do.
You must get such great inspiration.
What do you mean?

5

She'd need to insulate
that roof, double-glaze
her windows, and what about
the seat of her pants? She'll need
a jockey's bollocks to survive
the long nights of doubt, the long
knives of auto-dissection, the
wearisome 'I' in isolation.

6

You think they're following you
then you look back but
there's no one there.

7

Building bridges, burning them,
going a bridge too far – for now
no need to bridge the gap between

island
        &   home.

Time enough for tomorrow
tomorrow.

8

When she decides
to leave
there will be nothing
to be afraid of,

nothing that
bounds her front
and back, the nothing
that is everything there is.

OUT OF KILTER
for Mike Merchant

Get your horizon straight, the photographer said,
dismissing my exquisite picture with four words.

And now, although I know Earth's surface curves
I cannot leave the house, or go to bed, without

first sizing up the distance, right and left, of
sea to sky or sky to shore. Away from home,

I search for horizontal lines to take
my bearings from: the roofs of houses, a well-

clipped hedge, wires
                              strung
                                        between old poles

linking farm   to barn,
                    scraps of voice still snagged

in the sagging cables,
                              swifts littering the sky with

tipsy quadrants
                    and the noon sun pressing down,

plumb to the tilted ground
                              beneath my feet.

A QUESTION OF PITCH

The swallow outside my open window chatters
with other invisible birds, an urgent long message
ending in rapid-fire clicks

and soon more birds are fleshed out by sunlight,
skelfed from the undergrowth in slivers
of orange and gold, unfamiliar to me

but not to the white cat
vigilant, impassive
unmoved by the dull thud of falling figs

or my sudden arrival which she notes
with the flick of an ear
that's deaf

to the ambulance, the motorbike high
as a hornet's whine or the child
just home from school already practising piano

a handful of notes
over and over
like the sparrows'

and none of them entirely in tune.

PIECES OF STRING

It is impractical to use the same unit for the distance between two
cities and the length of a needle.

– Wikipedia.org

Each evening I shake out my day,
contrive a means to measure up
the hours I've travelled, try
to calculate the weight or shape,
the height, the depth, the very substance
of anything I met along the way.

I fail. I'll tell you straight, I fail.

The path to morning is a broken line
tracing the spine of a country road
meandering through fog, a rain-drenched
map, nothing left to set my compass by,
to gauge how far I've come or remind me
of anything I met along the way.

                    Clocks aren't much use
on edgeless days. Blurred numbers roll
like a throw of unmarked dice, ricochet
from the baffled corners of the house,
conjuring the handless clock in
Bergman's *Wild Strawberries*, a film
my parents brought me to when I was ten

– in an old man's dream, a coffin opens
as it falls from a horse-drawn hearse;
a hand emerges, the old man's own;
it reaches up and tries to haul him back.
A no-frills encounter with time's treachery
I was too young to understand, or forget.

ALARM

A faint whistle, a silver whisper,
a secret shared in the night. I saw
snow, white sheets stretched under
sentinel trees, the moon above,
a faint breeze in high branches.

When the whistle grew to a whine
I turned in the bed, buried my head
under pillows. I watched wolves stalk
in single file, their paw prints even as
holes in a flute, each rough-pelted creature
making a little leap as it drew its paws up
out of the depth of the snow.

                    With each leap
a sudden shriek, shriller, louder now,
loud enough to cause me to sit up, stare
into the dark, hear the scarlet wail,
                              smell smoke.

What's in a Name

In the beginning
a mouthful of sounds,
a handful of letters,
the tyranny of words.

A word was said,
and it was. Was said
alchemy and all around
May-warm broom flowered,
heady with sweet honey-gold.

Was thought *broom*, and then said,
and fragrant petals fell, twigs
scratched and turned brown, swept
the hearth where Cinderella moped.

Saw *scuttle* and then said it, heard
the hiss, the slither of snake.
Said *Apple!* Said *Out!*

So they left, mistaking
the word for the thing.
Literal as obedience
Eve opened a gate
that was no more than a word.
Adam locked it behind them.

OH SINNER MAN

Out of the blue
a sneaky draught
blew the door open

tumbled walls in a gust
of cosmic breath, a noxious
puff from god knows

where. And so we fell,
one by one, like weeping
beads of soldered lead,

dropped in an unmapped
zone where we stood
exposed as skinny dippers

caught in an island cove,
ashamed and shivering under
the searchlight's hunting probe.

WHAT WERE HER PARENTS THINKING WHEN THEY CALLED HER CASS?

It comes most nights now, the dream
she can't get rid of. It goes like this.

The staircase to the basement
opens like an aching throat, air
shunts her face and neck, she tests
her footing, falls, tumbles through hoarse
shadows. Her pupils pool, ears stretch
to gauge the silence.

Nothing.

Only darkness, louder than sound, time
slowed to no time. She's paused between
two worlds. She waits to surface, the way you wait
in supermarket car parks for the lift, the way
you wait for a parent to remember you.

And that's not all.

Last night it changed, it was as if she'd hit
a switch and rows of neon strip lights burst
the silence, flickered into dazzle, lit her
with the cruel fluorescence of a killing place.

She stood in an abandoned abattoir, steel hooks
idle, the tiles bright white. Somewhere water
ran. A clock began to tick. Her world had flipped
to future tense, the hooks began to sway, the rhythm
tachycardiac. And then the sudden cranking of a vast
machine, a slow robotic creature waking up.

Tonight she will not close her eyes.
Instead she'll walk the moonlit wood
behind the house. She'll watch the sky
drop stars through naked branches,
say a prayer.

LATE TREES
after Philip Larkin

The trees are standing still and grey
like ships unrigged and calcified;
their trunks shine ghostly at first light,
no breath or breeze to make them sway.

So what if they've already died
while we live on? Well, we'll die too.
Same golden sunsets, sparkling dew,
just no one on the mountainside.

It's past midday, the tall masts are silent stacks,
ravaged and reproachful as Gethsemane.
'You made us thus,' they seem to say,
'Go back, go back, go back.'

ON THE LENGTH OF THE DAY, OR THE NIGHT

No dogbark, no cockcrow, no crows.
No cars, no sounds from the sea.
No flies or mosquitoes. No lizards.
No cats, no magpies, no grizzled labrador
    folding onto his place in the yard.
No golden oriole ladling melody
    over the citrine sky.
No sparrow brigade tufting carpets,
    no mutiny brewing over low pay.
No mewling buzzard, its gull-cry
    at odds with the spread of its tapestry wings.
No swift swifts slicing the sky, working out theorems
    with compass and pencil,
    wondering why.
No housewifely house martin, stubby and efficient,
    apron tied as she dives home again, and again,
    and again to the gaping nest.
No handfuls of scops owls small in the night, invisible
    measurements, lonely beep-beeps, heart-
    stopping, breath-holding, testing the night
    for life.
No screeching screech owls, shredding
    the night sheet, ripping strips of
    nothing from nothing.
No petulant kestrels in the small stand of trees
    behind the square orange house.
No gang of hoopoes loitering on the tarmac of
    the potholed road, *poseurs* on the verge,
    beaks in a droop, crests at rest.
No woodpecker shrieking raucous affront,
    low-flown escape to the trees, stubby rotors
    fixed to the fat cigar of its hurtling body.
No pigeons, no doves, no pied wagtails.
No black redstart's glowing cigarette
    barely visible in leaf shadow. No blackbirds.

No trill of robin or wren. No tree creeper mousing
   up a tree.
No flurries of goldfinches. No anonymous shapes
   in the too many leaves.
No grating cicadas, no corncrakes.
No implacable commentary.

THIS WAS NOT THE DEAL

The deal was I die
and the world goes on and
on. The deal was that it was
everlasting.
           This is not
what I signed up for: a short
stretch on a finite surface,
mortal on a mortal planet.

The deal was it went on forever,
                 creating,
            sustaining,
                    regenerating a sphere
      of fire and forest, incessant
                rebirth
        mother / father / son & daughter
        goose / gander / gosling
        mare / stallion / foal
        bull / cow / calf
        mountain
        stream
        river
        sea.

Begat, begat, begat.
That was the deal, right?
A world without end.
Amen.

Now horses paw the stable floor,
dust rises from their feed, skin drapes
their ribs like threadbare blankets,
flames kindle in the recess of their
plumbless eyes. They need no sign.

SPIN CYCLE

i

I'm standing in a glow of screens
in the shop where I have come to buy
a common kettle. Words spew,
fragments fall, acronyms call out
to missing letters, commas
cling to shattered syllables,
specks of twisted meaning
fine as ash. Dust settles
on white surfaces
where fish now rise
to gob the coating,
mouths hinged in awful parody,
obscene O O Os ...
then down into the mud
to wait for the return of light,
for the sky itself to lift.

ii

In a forgotten valley
villagers are on high alert:
they watch the sky,
herd sheep and hens,
call their dogs and children
to the safety of the biggest barn;
they check their stores, harvests
gathered in, prayed over.
Fathers sing soft and low,
soothe the woken child,
trust the storm erupting
from behind the mountain
will not come their way,
that they will remain
forgotten, as brute words
spin in their relentless cycle,
relentless as the rain
that starts to fall.

WOOL FOR WEAVING

That was the year thread went scarce,
yarn for binding, mending, fixing;
wire was hard to come by, thin
rope or twine in skeins and hanks.

The year after that, seams
burst open, soles came away
from their uppers; it was the year
of no containment when seas over-
flowed with plastic, when

fish choked on the finger bones of
children, and beach attendants
went on strike because the dead
would not pay; that year
they began to bottle tears,
archive mothers' cries.

SUCH SILENCE
SHE FELL
INTO

in memory of
Geraldine Kirby
1882–1930

My grandmother was just three when her mother died giving birth to a baby sister. My great grandmother's first name was Geraldine and the name was passed to the newborn child. In turn, it was given to me.

Great-aunt Geraldine was never talked about when we were children, not in my hearing at any rate. Her father, Michael Kirby, was a 'shoe merchant' in Cork City, her mother's maiden name was Griffin. Her own life remains a mystery. I know only fragments: that she was a talented pianist, a performer and teacher, Licentiate of the Royal Academy of Music, London; that she had been engaged to be married but broke it off; and that at some point she was governess to a military family posted in Warsaw.

I have a leather suitcase that was hers and just one photograph, with *Rouen, May 1930* written on the back. That was the year she took her life. She died on 20 October 1930 in lodgings in Stansted, Essex – though why she was living there, or how she was earning her living at the time, history does not relate. The death certificate is stark: *Cause of death – coal gas poisoning due to her placing her head in a gas oven. Suicide while of unsound mind.*

because wind, because rain
because skin over bone
because night worn thin

because web
because fabric
because blanket

because patchwork quilt
because stitch, stitch, stitch
because love, because story

because linked arms, stout legs
because holding
because held

because graveyards so full
because with us forever
because we will not forget

because human bridge
because love
because story

The graveyard's expectant
as an empty stage, but
there's no guarantee
they'll dance tonight.

We let on we're not scared,
tell each other stories
– your family, mine –
the TB, the suicides,

the longest living and
the soonest dead. We try
to calculate the density of
corpses, cubic meters, multiples of

bones, the depths they must descend to.
We wrap our minds
round Earth's broad girth,
make lists of wars, add to the bony heap of

life's ordinary debris.
We sit bone white under
a mandible moon.
Quiet as death.

And still no clickety-clack,
no clatter,
no clash.

As if time was distance
I see you drift out to sea
on an absence of years.

As if distance was time
I measure the years
that separate your life from mine.

As if time and distance
did not exist, I imagine us
sitting in silence side by side.

nothing to say that isn't

nothing to say

how close

the sacred is to scared

when edges fray   time
evaporates   sense dissolves

dizzy whiteout

no hold
on the wind now

the gaps
need stopping up or the sand
will flow out
& away

A clear sky
and the lateral spill of light
over fields, reeds and sea.
Sun laid down like gold leaf.

That day in the woods
when they had all gone home
you had hidden too well
no one to find you, only owls
and a badger shuffling.

Break it up
    let it fall
        pick it up

        watch what shapes
           appear.

      Do it again
        and again.

Sun laid like gold leaf
over sloping fields
over surfaces of stone
and tumbled gable ends.

You still hidden.
Still unfound.
The boxes in the attic
above the bed.
The suitcase.

I lay your story
on the floor –

you start to hum
you are near.

(Sometimes when we wake
the weight of pain so heavy
we throw the blankets off).

The suitcase lay tongue-tied as a tomb. On rainy afternoons we'd dare each other up the cobwebbed stairs, thrill with shapes still blanketed in dark, our own familiar ghosts. A single dusty bulb, and out of broken boxes the grope of musty clothes. The ballerina winks an absent eye and then the game can start: my sister susurrates some hocus pocus prayer and one by one we drop to scabby knees, call up your spirit, great-aunt we never knew, the one they never talked about, your initials stamped in leather marble-hard.

Who knew your story?
Who remembers?

We looked and looked.
Why didn't you cry out?
We stayed after dark.
You didn't move.

old stories sift
and stir

riddled
by the unexpected

whispering
of voices

settle
into hollows

under ash –

Who was that woman
dressed all in white
looking down on the street
in the chill hours
of a winter's night
through moonlit shutter slats

like a girl in a film
dreaming the part
of a newly-wedded woman
shadow pooling
her delicate neck
eyes welled

remembering the mother
she never knew
stories of calving
the pain of her birth
a small body slithering
into rank straw

at the lowing cow's feet
a heifer too young
to know how to lick
to flip the raw pain
nudge it to its feet
in the unlit bedroom

of the seaside village
where she began to bleed
far from a doctor's help
leaving the infant
orphaned for life

A door
without keyhole or handle,
hinged to the entrance
of her heart.

A twist of rope,
rough wisps visible
against the fading light.

No one walks this way
for fear of hidden roots,
of sleeping curs roused
to frenzied barks.

A spider spins its web
between the bell pull and
the weathered door.

It sits and waits.
It watches.
It has time.

silence
becomes silk
on the last wheeze
of night

the s of sorry snakes
through the eye
of hollow self
slips

in forked tongue stitches
x by x
through the sampler's
muslin sheet
needle cotton
blood

She used to tell her pupils she could hear the stars.
The stars all sing, each one a different note.
But their parents found a way to stop her.

Grey noise they called it, worse than white.
For her and for the children who still could hear
this stellar song, music arcing the high night sky,

who, like her, sat still and smiled to hear
the pulsing echoes of a million, million years,
the peal and quiver of sharp diamond light,

for them they made the murk of grey – aural dust
to swirl and whisper, fill clean air with
drone enough to drown the music of the spheres.

In her dreams owls
drown, feathered

spectres,
swivelled moons.

She sees them shimmer, slip
through twilit murk, do back-
flips, slo-mo somersaults.

She follows them down
to say she is sorry,
all she wants is

to watch them glide
from the haggard to the

small oak wood; learn again
the old ways of silence.

She goes back to
the seaside house
on a windless winter's day.

Bats dangle
from the kitchen beams,
patient leathered souls.

She strokes the silence, pulls it round her,
shoulders it through fractured door frames
as she ghosts from room to room.

Echoes dance in unremembered corners, jig her
from the shiver of her ageing skin.
The still air fills her ears.

By dawn she's fallen back onto
a featherbed of incremental sound:
dogs have set each other off,

cockerels too,
that merely stretch their necks to announce
the immanence of a morning where

the spider's web
so patiently constructed
now hangs in tatters.

like ash
or the fallout of angels

snow
in feeble flurries

textbook atoms
spinning

jackdaws scrap
above the roof

dispute
the only chimney

left to nest in
retreat

to inky branches
black featherfall

Black bees/white noise
in the hollow trunk
of the old plane tree
below the window;

everything here so
familiar/unfamiliar,
or is it that she has forgotten
the way moonlight

can skewer the bedroom
through a shutter crack,
the crepitation of tyres
over sand-crush and pebbles,

the discreet/indiscreet dawn
departure of a lover, the illusion
of being unseen, thinned dark
poor cover when dogs snarl

as they doze and a streak of
black cat sleeks from under
the gangling lavender, un-
leashes a memory,

an out-of-body déjà vu,
impossible to capture
from the widening delta
of the past.

Far out on night's ocean
she feels the surge
of the sea,

the bang and slap
of the keel in the trough
of a wave,

feels the sting
of salt as it lashes
her face

but her eyes are
sealed tight
with the scales of

the hundreds of fish
she has gutted, a mean
little knife still gripped

in her hand. She arches
her back, strains
to break loose

of the diesel stench,
swim to calm
waters, wake.

how busy the birds are
– the still morning air
thickened with wings –

the jackdaws' scrambling
louder than ever – heavy
black petticoat flaps –

what is the meaning of this
invasion – these scissors that
stab – these rapiers drawn –

her silence unnerves her –
ripped up and shredded
– it flies like ticker tape

falls like litter –
no one to talk to
– not even herself

Her tongue explodes // crimson words // spray confetti
of no sense // at all // the phone protests // she shuts
the flow // it works its way back up // circuitous
journey // eardrum to anvil to stirrup // round and
round the cochlea's loops and tubes // until it's all
buzz and sizzle // a daze of black wire // a seethe of
fire // crackle and flash // short fizzle // (…) // but still
the pulse travels on circuits of copper and skin // the
fire still unravels //

She holds her breath, listens closely,
prepares to dive into the narrow space
where noise is not, the rift in time
that opens instants before a concert starts,
the hidden place where silence is distilled.

This is a moment of neither then nor
now, when forest leaves hang dumb, birds
sleep, heads tucked beneath their wings,
their feathers settled smoothly layer on layer.
This is where she would make her home,

in a silence sleek as silk, limpid
as truth, or the absence of pain.
If she gets her timing right she'll
plunge in, vanish into that brief lull,
those few mute moments.

Out in the yard
beyond the ladders and scaffolding
the sheets of garden trellis

    behind the piled up bags of compost
    the bales of briquettes and
    sacks of coal

before you get
to the hen coop
and the wooden sheds

    that's where she found it
    a dog kennel
    square and sturdy

its door open and
just the right size
so she stooped down

    crawled in
    curled up
    laid her head

on her neatly
folded hands
and slept.

Pour Out the Dark

II

DARKNESS CANNOT DRIVE OUT DARKNESS
– Martin Luther King Jr.

As long as there are wolves
there will be sheep

As long as there is a moon
there will be lovers

As long as there is wind
there will be leaves

As long as there are thrushes
there will be snails

As long as there is smoke
there will be fire

As long as there is outrage
there will be hope

As long as there is death
there will be life

As long as there is killing
there must be justice

MAKING A FIST

i.m. Jamal Khashoggi

Fingers never looked so beautiful as mine,
flexing to support a plain black pen
poised to make the shapes required
to convey a sickened sense of horror
on learning how a man had all his digits
severed, was slowly done to death, dismembered
and disposed of god knows where.

Never have four fingers and a thumb appeared
so precious, no pen as strong as mine. I angle
the age-old weapon like a dart, watch as
black gloved ink flows down the page in measured
curlicues, tempered by the teamwork of my hand.
Until the work is done and ten frail fingers rest
helpless on the blackened page, like fists undone.

PAPER BAGS

I've just read Yannis Ritsos' lines
about a group of men
who faced the firing squad.

Their last request: *a paper bag apiece.*
When the guns were raised,
before the shots, in a ruse

to neutralise the blast
they blew into the bags,
burst them on the brick façade

then dropped like stones.
We blew up paper bags as children,
burst them, just for fun.

BULLY BOY

While other children
screamed and raced
around the garden

he worried
who would pick him
when the games began

follow my leader
stick a tail on the donkey
musical chairs

braced for rejection
he'd volunteer
to have a scarf

tied tightly round
his eyes
for *blind man's buff*

then stand
the centre of the rumpus
as noises fell away

and he explored
the inside of his head
where everything went quiet

like when he slid his whole face
underwater
in the bath

he felt a power well up
then breached the silence
suddenly

dealt out
rough justice
on the scattering room

THEY COME AND THEY GO
Tuam 1925–1960

the fathers
the brothers
the uncles
the cousins
the neighbours
the priests

the sweethearts
the hardhearts
the bravehearts
the fainthearts
the broken
                hearts

the bighearted
the lighthearted
the halfhearted
the heavyhearted
the warm and coldhearted

liars and drunks and wheedlers
smooth-talking flatterers

soft-talking blaggards
ugly-tongued slaggers

tinkerstailorssoldierssailors
richmenpoormenbeggarmen

thieves

the men
who fathered
the children
who died.

KESTREL

A synchronised swimmer
        and none but herself
to be in sync with;
        the air is water and
she treads it, scours
        earth's barrel bottom
for anything that moves.

January light is harsh and clear,
        each shadow and contour
of vole or shrew
        etched in contrast,
caught in the crosshairs
        of the skydiver's desire.

The crew-cut stubble's short,
        only stands of reeds
give camouflage and cover;
        the mice are hungry too,
they creep like lice
        between wasted blades.

AFTER DRAWINGS BY JUSEPE DE RIBERA

It isn't that the evil thing wins – it never will
– but that it doesn't die.

                    – John Steinbeck

Workmen sort out
the technical difficulties
of crucifying St Peter
upside down,
as if calculating

how to attach a piano
with pulley and ropes
and raise it to the upper floor
of a rich man's house.
No easy job.

St Bartholomew
is being flayed alive,
lashed loosely to a tree. See
the unkempt crew, the
diligence of the master

butcher tasked with
filleting the muscles
of the apostle's upper arm,
a knife clenched between
his teeth, his knees

gently bent, looking
for all the world
like a seamstress working
on a dressmaker's dummy,
her mouth bristled with pins.

REQUEST
Algiers, 1976

The moment still scalds after all these years,
opening the door to find you there with flowers,
the sun behind your head, heat and dust
gusting into my flat, a look of fear –
Palestine, home lost, and now this plea
to give you a pass in your final English test.

A small request. I have a home,
a job, firm ground beneath my feet.
Surely not too much to ask?
I stand on the threshold of my first floor flat,
look at my feet. The moment still scalds.
The sun behind your head. The dust. The heat.

MEMO TO MINISTERS RESPONSIBLE FOR HOUSING
AND IMMIGRATION

Remember that day
driving home
in fog,

the stretch of road
unrecognisable,
trees appearing
where there were none.

Remember the fear
in that moment
of not knowing.

AS MY DAUGHTER FLIES NORTH I EXAMINE MY FEAR
for Lisa

All night I cup you
in my feathered hands and
picture in the studded sky

a silver bird, cold carcass,
you slumbering in the hum,
the cool penumbra,

hushed comfort of the stewards'
slender palms. This morning
as I lean into the wind

a kestrel rides a fold of pillowed
air, buoyed up by nothing but
its own intent, its feathers

spread to steer and hold, trust
the instinct it was born with;
six whoopers suddenly above me,

a honking contrail quaffing sun,
wings in steady semaphore
to the unfledged world.

They land on liquid runways,
knead the water, glide to silken
stops. Trust us, they seem to say,

your stiff-winged bird will make
soft landing: we taught you
all you know of flight.

SHORT NIGHTS, CHOPPY SEAS
for Jean Tuomey

The wind has chipped
        the sea like delph,
thrashed and flayed it
            to worked hide.
It has nothing more to say
        to me today
            and turns its rugged back.
I pull the blind,
        go in search of sleep instead.
            All through these short,
long nights I wake and toss
        and wake again, my bed
            a floundering raft,
beached at last in the slow linger
            of returning light,
                the thinning chorus of birds.
    My body buzzed all night,
        ache hummed through me
like an electric fence.
        I lie in the relief of dawn,
                listen for a faint *tik-tik*,
proof the current flows,
                    taking me back
        to how we used to dare each other,
            how from the safety
of the longest stem of grass
        we'd apprehend the bite
            of the unseen beast,
                jumping back and squealing
at the slightest kick, or dropping
        stalk after stalk
        before they so much as touched the wire.
        Which led my early morning wakefulness
to thoughts of touch,

how all through long weeks
        and months we did without,
how when we thought it safe again
        we reached out cautious hands,
        slowly opened
        famished arms,
half fearful of the pent-up charge.

My Flesh Peels Back Some Autumn Days

like bark, turns on itself with worry
and the dread of death. Late October
I set out for the blazing beech wood,

my spent joints jarring, chin skin loose
as a chameleon's, my powers of disappearing,
of blending into leaf swirl, just as good.

Now watch my amber eyes, how they flicker
and all they see: Xanadu's *sunny spots* lie
dull beside the opulent complexity of

shantung falls, cascades of radiance,
the welter of gyrating leaves. Out here –
skin shed and flesh repaired – I live

St Brigid Dreams of the Arrival of Spring

deep in her skull
a bud is forming
a bird has nested
in her wasted chest

small twigs tickle
eggs speckle the moss
(she says these things
says she sees them

in the curtained dark)
deep in her nest
a flower may open
a tulip black as

the year's been long
she says it's hiding
its yellow tongue
biding its time

to part its petals
surprise the brightening
room with light
pour out the dark

TAKE IT SLOW
for Bob Hull

The way to be slow is not difficult. Wait for the sun. Keep
your eye on the ball. Wear sunglasses. Use factor fifty.
Leave the other half open to chance: a fracas in the garden,
birds guarding their nests, the usual hoo-ha, magpies
under attack, tails vertical as they dance the phone wire
and jackdaws swerve and swoop; at the gate an Italian
tourist, *nel mezzo del cammin,* heading the wrong way; an
unfranked letter from an old friend in England, eyesight
failing, handwriting too, a beautiful scatter of black marks
over four pages, bird tracks, hieroglyphs only partly
decipherable and all the more arresting for that. Be
detained on the garden bench, the thick cream pages
releasing their meaning nice and slow, and hours to go
before sundown sends a shiver through the long May day.

MAPPING THE WAY BACK

When all our systems fail, when satellites
fall to earth like birds – and birds fall, too –

when darkness falls, as some old holy men
have warned it may, then we will have to learn

new languages, words like 'candle', 'kindling',
'neighbourhood', the length of 'an Irish mile'.

Museums will proffer foot-powered lathes, wind-up
gramophones, black discs giving voice to quavering

music as they spin. In our town, one man's
house will be more frequented than a church in

years gone by – those buildings long destroyed or
used to house the homeless and the poor. Here,

in the soft-toned downwash of a wind-powered
standard lamp, he'll supervise the copying

of what he names 'maps'. He'll measure out each
shuffling person's head-bent drawing time by

a small round object that glimmers as he
draws it from a pocket near his heart and

which he sometimes fiddles with, twisting
a tiny button with a rasping sound. These

'maps' he'll lovingly release from long brown
tubes, eliciting from each of us some

clues to where we come from, where each lives,
forcing us to rack our brains for some old

feature, antique remnant – graveyard, holy
well or ruined barracks – an unlikely

stone or monument, long gone but real still
to grandparents in their dotage, locals

channelling strange pictures from the past.
Once found, we'll trace the shapes to crumpled sheets

of grey-green paper the man has made:
fields and houses, streets or highways as they

used to be. Next day, out in the half-light
of the sun at noon, you'll see us all: each

clutching a slip of magic, their own 'map',
soul passport, precious ticket back to Time.

ACKNOWLEDGEMENTS

Acknowledgements are due to the editors of the following publications or sites where some of these poems, or versions of them, first appeared:

Abridged, Aesthetica Creative Writing Annual 2019, Crannóg, Cyphers, Poetry Ireland Review, The Interpreter's House, The Irish Times, The North, The Stinging Fly, The Stony Thursday Book, Write Where We Are Now

'Making a Fist' was commended in the 2019 Gregory O'Donoghue International Poetry Competition

'Request' was shortlisted for the Strokestown International Poetry Competition in 2015

'As My Daughter Flies North I Examine My Fear' was shortlisted for the Strokestown International Poetry Competition in 2019

'Oh Sinner Man' was shortlisted for the Fish Lockdown Poetry Competition 2020

An earlier version of 'Such Silence She Fell Into' was shortlisted for the Fool for Poetry chapbook competition 2019

Radio:
'St Brigid Dreams of the Arrival of Spring' was broadcast on RTÉ's *Sunday Miscellany* on 28/01/18

'*because wind, because rain*' was broadcast on RTÉ's *Sunday Miscellany* on 02/02/20

'Test' was broadcast on RTÉ's *Sunday Miscellany* on 22/03/20

Poems have also appeared, or will appear, in the following anthologies:
Something About Home: New Writing on Migration and Belonging, ed. Liam Harte (Geography Publications, 2017)

Reading the Future: New Writing from Ireland, ed. Alan Hayes (Arlen House/Hodges Figgis, 2018)

Strokestown Poetry Anthology 3 (2019)

Empty House: Climate Change Anthology, ed. Nessa O'Mahony and Alice Kinsella (Doire, 2021)

'Mapping the Way Back' was written as part of the Benchmarks project, Linenhall Arts Centre, Castlebar, facilitated by Mike McCormack, October 2019

In 'Paper Bags' I have quoted from David Harsent, *In Secret: Versions of Yannis Ritsos* (Enitharmon Editions, 2012)

Warmest thanks to Aoife Casby and John Murphy for their continuing poetry conversations and for keeping me on my toes. Thank you to Jane Clarke, Ted Deppe, Mags Duffy, Elaine Feeney and Mike McCormack who all took time with the manuscript at various stages. And to publisher Alan Hayes – once again, thanks.

ABOUT THE AUTHOR

Geraldine Mitchell was born in Dublin. For more than twenty years she lived in France, Algeria and Spain, working as a teacher and freelance journalist, before returning to Ireland. Since 2000 she has lived on the County Mayo coast.

She won the Patrick Kavanagh Award for her debut collection, *World Without Maps* (Arlen House, 2011), followed by *Of Birds and Bones* in 2014 and *Mountains for Breakfast* in 2017. *Mute/Unmute* is her fourth collection.

Mitchell is also the author of two novels for young people, *Welcoming the French* (Attic Press, 1992) and *Escape to the West* (Attic Press, 1994), and a biography, *Deeds Not Words: The Life and Work of Muriel Gahan* (TownHouse, 1997).

www.geraldinemitchell.net